A Church Girl's Story...The Path to No Return

By

Cora S. Fells

A Church Girl's Story… The Path to No Return

Copyright © 2020, Cora S. Fells

All rights reserved. No part of this book may be reproduced or transmitted in any form or by any means without written permission from the author.

ISBN: 978-164713-68-71

Dedication

To my younger self and children. You made this possible and I am forever thankful…

My Dearest Younger Cora:

I apologize to you, I did not treat you as you deserved and I should have put you first. I loved everyone except you! I was so caught up in what people thought about me, but never stopped to consider what you would think of me... Would you, at 35 years old be so upset with the things I allowed to happen to you? Or, would you see things how I see them now?

You are amazing… and I tainted you with men who used and abused what should have been preserved for our husband. Know this, I finally love you and understand that everything happens for a reason. I will no longer let dark paths and past endeavors be apart of our future. We got this! Thank you for not quitting, I admire that about you. You were so young and endured so many unfortunate events… but you still kept a smile on your face!

Now, I know why I'm so strong; you built me for this. I love you and I love me – first! I no longer take "NO" as an option... because I realize that I can do all things through Christ who strengthens me!

I Love You,

A stronger, Wiser and More Beautiful Cora

My Beloved Children:

Peypey and Kenzie both of you rock! I love the air you breathe and if it weren't for you, I wouldn't be here! Whether you know it or not, you kept the fire burning inside me, and you all taught me the right way to love. I'm so proud of both of you! You're smart and loving just like mommy. I cannot thank you enough for loving me and being here for me. I will always appreciate those perfect hugs and the perfect words both of you said to me when I was down. Keep being great!

Love Always,

Mommy

Table of Contents

Introduction v

Chapters

1: Born into Crack 1

2: Growing Up Church Style 6

3: Expect the Unexpected 13

4: Battered but Not Scorned 20

5: It Could Have Been Me 31

6: The Love of Revenge 35

7: The Will to Live Again 41

8: Recovery 45

9: New Beginnings 49

10: Letters to My Beloveds 53

Introduction

A Church Girl's Story... Path to No Return navigates the paths I wandered. The paths that broke me, crushed me, and ultimately rebuilt and shaped me into the phenomenal woman I am now. I share my story and truths regarding the lifestyle I lived while being hurt by several different situations; several of these situations were a result of my brokenness and the choices I made.

Nevertheless, my sole purpose for sharing my truth(s) is to encourage readers and let them know that they can overcome any situation; whether they were born into it or if life seemingly dealt them an unfair hand. God is in full control and He has the final say concerning our lives.

I pray this book inspires numerous young men and women that may be headed down the wrong path. Trust and believe, if I made it you can too! In fact, my declaration for every reader is, no matter what path(s) you've traveled so far, you will walk into a place of light… where peace, love, and abundant blessings await!

This book is also a personal vow to myself; that my past will not dictate my future and there are paths I will never tread again… because I've learned my lessons and I love me too much!

Chapter 1

Born into Crack

Can you imagine being born on drugs? Do you believe that although I NEVER physically touched drugs with my own hands…? I was addicted; this is almost an unbelievable truth!

My name is Cora Shanelle Fells, I was born on December 15th, 1984. It was a cold December night… just when my mom *thought* she was about to get "another hit," Boom! Labor pains started. Due to her condition she was rushed to a local hospital in Gainesville, Florida.

There I was a beautiful baby girl, perfectly innocent but addicted not to a drug that had taken the streets of Palatka, Florida by storm. Even then, God had a plan for my life!

When I was just a few days old, my grandma took me and my other 4 siblings into her home. My mother could not properly take care of us anymore. I suffered and endured several medical complications because of my mother's drug use. Even in this, I often wondered how could my momma leave me? Did she love me? Was I unworthy of her love and affection? These questions bombarded my mind almost daily. As I grew older, I realized something much more powerful prompted my questioning.

Meet My Father

He strolled down 11th street in a 3-piece suit looking "extra fly?" Who was this man…? It was evident that he was not from Palatka. He had captured my mom's complete attention. She admitted, that initially my daddy was just her "sugar daddy." There was a drastic age difference between them.

After a few weeks of coming back and forth to Palatka, their fling came to a screeching halt, when my mother realized she was pregnant... *with me*. Eventually, my mom found out why my father's visits were consistently short-lived. He had a wife and step children... an entire family and a "settled life." Poppa was obviously a "rolling-stone."

I am my father's *only* biological child. However, in reality... he had a whole family that he dipped back and forth from every time he met up with my mom. I don't think he was ready for the unexpected news from my mom, "I'M PREGNANT!"

His wife did not know I existed until I was 5 years old. My dad creeped into town to check on me whenever he could… but because he was married, he was unable to be an active part in my life. This caused expected distance between us, our relationship was not as close as it should have been.

At the tender age of eighteen, my dad and I tried to rekindle our relationship, it was too late… the damage had been done. He passed away a few years later, and I was left with too many unanswered questions… because I never worked up enough courage to ask. When he died, the closure I yearned for was no longer accessible.

My father's death taught me that sometimes, the people we love most may not love us the same. It hurt me to know, that a man who wasn't devoted to me, needed me. He treated badly and I had to lay him to rest.

I barely knew him… I almost disliked him. I was confused and hurt as I stared at his lifeless body during the funeral. "Why didn't he love me?" I felt the awakening of a cold-hearted beast within me.

Chapter 2

Growing up Church Style

Growing up, I was affectionately known as "the pastor's granddaughter." It was a blessing and a curse at the same time! I hated that *everyone* expected me to be "perfect." However, even if f I could change anything... I wouldn't!

My grandmother tried her best to make my life as a child as easy as possible. I know she carried the heartbreaking agony of my mother's drug addiction. Grandma took me to church conventions with her all across the United States... if I didn't know anything else, I *knew* church!

Unfortunately, no matter how hard my grandma tried... she couldn't fill the heavy void in my life. Mothers are irreplaceable. I was lost and I felt as if I couldn't tell anyone how I really felt. Maybe, I was ashamed and for some reason, I thought no one could really understand. I believed I would be judged and my strength as a child was admittedly non-existent.

At the time, I thought if no one else can help me... my grandma can! To me, she was like superwoman. I witnessed her help countless people from the church with *all* of their problems. People were slain in the spirit and the holy ghost move like never before! Demons were cast out people and they were *seemingly* set free! With great sincerity, I prayed and hoped for my grandmother to *help my mom*! Surely, she could at least do that... if not for my mom, couldn't she do it for her grandchildren?

I often stared at the church doors, hoping that my mother would walk through them, and give her life to God. I knew He could help her… if no one else could.

The church life showed me *a lot*… some things were good and some things were bad. I swept into my teenage years fairly quickly; and my mom's drug habit had her the same size as me. My grandma purchased all the name brand clothes and I stayed dressed in the latest styles.

Quite frequently, my mom came to Grandma's house to shower, then she'd change into *my* school clothes, and go traipsing right back to eleventh street with *my* clothes on. I cried my eyes out until my grandma bought more clothes for me. I tried so hard to hide my belongings, but my mom's drug addiction had her scavenging for them until she found what she came for... she often took other valuables to get her drugs.

This made me upset and I lashed out badly towards family members and anyone else who crossed my path. My anger and attitude problems were terrible! I needed my mom and she didn't understand that. I behaved so badly, that my family didn't want me at their homes or around their children. They didn't want my "bad ways" to rub off on them. I knew I had to change... but at the time I could only focus on *my* pain.

My tenth-grade year, was probably my worst year ever growing up! All the other years I "successfully" hid who my mother was... but at this point I couldn't.

There was a local prostitution sting and my Mother was on the front page serving the ugliest mug shot available! I could have gone through the walls of Palatka High School! It seemed as though every student in the school had a newspaper in their hands.

I couldn't help but hear the whispers, "That's Cora's mom...!" and then the laughter erupted down the hallways from my peers. I hid in the bathroom and cried! I gathered myself and darted to the front office to call my grandma. I begged her to pick me up as quickly as possible! She came swiftly because she knew I needed her.

Shortly after that my mother went to court [as she often did], but the judge had grown tired of seeing her and decided to sentence her to five years in prison! My heart sank, I wanted her to get better but not this way. At least I was able see her every other day come in and out of grandma's house! But NOT prison! I was terrified for her and my teenage years were such a crucial time for me.

She missed all the "important things" in my life… being on homecoming court and going to the dance in my beautiful baby blue dress [I looked like a princess]. Let's not forget prom night in my dazzling red dress. And of course, my biggest day ever… Graduation! I received my diploma and knowing she was not in the stands broke my heart.

How could I go through this, I often cried to God? Even though all these things were going on, I managed to keep one thing… and that was my virginity. Well, at least until graduation.

A few weeks after graduation I started having sex with my high school boyfriend. We both were inexperienced and we tried all new sexual activities on each other. We dated a few years, then he went off to college. The first year was okay but I knew he had found someone who was more experienced and forgot all about little ole me in Palatka. This was the beginning of my search for love in *all the wrong places*!

Chapter 3

Expect the Unexpected

Life as I knew it was turned for the worst, I hit the club scene at least three times a week. I went to church on Friday nights... then I quickly changed into club clothes and raced up I-95 to meet up with my friends and party the night away!

I was known as Ms. Palatka, because I changed my name when I went out of the city! But I surely represented Palatka, so people knew where the "fine-slim girl" was from. I was only eighteen, but going to the club every week made me a pretty popular face! So, I was able to sway my way right into the club with my slim shape *for free*.

One night, I met this girl and we became friends. Her brother was a promoter too. Bingo!!! I was guaranteed a pass in that night. I was clubbing meeting different guys and since my high school sweetheart had gone off to college in Tallahassee... no one kept tabs on me! Besides, I was convinced he was doing his own thing.

I met different types of men and one night came across this really nice-looking guy. He had asked me to dance, we talked and exchanged numbers. He was a college student [or so I thought]. After a few weeks of meeting at the club, he asked me to come his place... I went, and to my surprise he led me to the north side of Jacksonville. I was petrified!

The guy and his friends were renting an old raggedy-looking house… it almost appeared condemned, that place was definitely on its last legs. I thought to myself, "What have I gotten myself into!?!" I was at a whole "Trap House." How I did end up here? "Oh Lord!" What have I gotten my "green-naïve" self into?

I calmed myself down because Mr. Good-Looking seemed to be protective and he intrigued me. I wanted to get to know him better, so I went inside the house. As the night progressed, I saw people come in and out the house with drugs and money. I was scared but my "new-boo" assured me that I would be ok.

We went into the room and "talked…" the situation escalated quickly!

He asked, "Have you ever made love?" I was barely twenty years old… so I said, "Of course not!" Mr. Good-looking was older and he caressed my body oh so gently! I had never felt like *that* and he whisked me away on the ride of my life! I was so inexperienced, so this felt amazing to me… my body was on a wonder drug. It was like drunkenness overwhelmed with extreme lust! It was something I felt only once in my lifetime.

We started seeing each other weekly and my real boyfriend faded away. He was so far away, that the saying, "*Out of sight out of mind*" really hit home as time passed. I was on my way to being a "certified trap queen" [or so I thought].

One day "my boo" sent me off on a shopping spree and told me to spend whatever! I did just that…when I was headed back to his home, I saw police cars from a mile away! The house was being raided. Oh God! What was I going do?!

I passed by slowly like I didn't know them… I saw "him" in the back of a police car and he signaled to me to keep driving! I couldn't get to Palatka fast enough… I never heard from him again! Maybe that was the thing… I wanted my brief "trap queen" moments to fade away as quickly as they came.

As I approached my twenty-first birthday, I was too excited to bring in my birthday "club style!" I was pretty popular by this time, and everywhere I turned *that* night... someone wanted to buy me a drink! I got so drunk I threw up all over myself and the club. I was so embarrassed; I ended my night vowing I would never drink again.

I eased up on the club scene when I met another Mr. Wrong, he was a local drug dealer. Yes, the excitement of the last one had me almost addicted to the toxicity. He was a different type though... he worked a nine to five job and his mother was a missionary at one of the local churches! How he ended up a drug dealer beat me... your guess is as good as mine!

We started a romantic relationship; we became closer and closer. I wanted more but he assured me he wasn't ready and I agreed and remain friends. However, in all honesty I wanted more... but he wouldn't give me that.

There I was... another failed relationship and I was going nowhere, *fast*. We spent months together and me and my high school boyfriend had called it quits... *completely!* So, I spent most of my nights trying to figure out the direction of my life. I really wanted to wait on my second "Mr. Wrong" to be ready... but months went by and then one day I ran into...

Chapter 4

Battered but Not Scorned

Young wild and free, I was so sadly mistaken! One night I pulled up at a local gas station. I noticed a tall handsome man; he was clean-shaven and well put together. I brushed my hair and put on some lip gloss in hopes that he'd notice me. I got out of the car and walked past him as if I was disinterested, but in reality, I was praying that he said hello. Then he spoke…

"Hey what's up? What's your name?" "Cora," I quickly replied. He said I looked like a nice young lady and he asked for my number. I pondered for a minute and then said yes… He wasn't just a ride; he was whole other level!

Our first date was not really a date. He picked me up from my grandma's house, and we went for a ride; he never said where we were going, but just the adventure had me excited.

We drove around for a couple of hours and grabbed a bite to eat. We talked and he seemed so perfect. He had a job, a car, and was well put together, but boy was I fooled.

I met him in the beginning of the month and by the end of that same month we were moving into our first apartment together. Everything happened so fast and, in my mind… he had stepped up to the plate when no-one else did! Therefore, I believed we were *destined* to be.

After the move in, I realized I didn't really get to know him… the dynamic of our "relationship" changed rapidly. One night, we decided to have a conversation. I asked the *really* important questions, the questions my lust caused me to overlook.

He dropped an atomic bomb on me… I literally saw explosions before my eyes! He confessed that he had been married before and had a total of eight children, my heart stopped and dropped! What had my 21-year-old-self gotten into? He also told me he had served a few prison terms but he insisted he was a changed man.

"How could I be so naïve," I thought to myself? Why didn't I ask all these questions before?" Now, I am living with this man!?! But... I was too *in love* by this time. This church girl whose life seemed so perfect had turned for a tragic end. I never saw it coming.

Life moved fairly quickly during these years; everything was okay until the second year. We had moved into another place and one night while we ate dinner, he looked at me and said, "Cora you are pregnant!" I quickly assured him that I wasn't and told him to get that out of his head. But he insisted I was and that I should go to the doctor.

So, the next day, I went to the doctor. I didn't tell anyone my plans. There I was... all alone, waiting for the doctor to come in. The words I didn't want to hear, invaded my mind loud and clear,

"Congratulations Ms. Fells, you are having a baby." Huh? He was right! Maybe he could sense it? He already had a football team and there I was adding *another* team member.

I went home and told him the news [he already knew]. Initially, he seemed so excited but a few months into the pregnancy his mannerisms changed. He started staying out late…and stopped paying attention to me. I angrily thought, "Oh no, this man done trapped me and now he is acting like he no longer wants me!" Rumors had floated around about him seeing other women but I never asked him about "the other women" until I got pregnant; maybe the hormones had me insecure…

One night I confronted him, and that's when *it* started. I was about three months pregnant and a *"simple question"* had me on the floor bleeding and crying as he kicked me in my stomach and punched me in my face! While he violently pummeled me, he warned me never to ask him any questions, *again*!

After he calmed down, he saw that I had not one, but two black eyes! I was in excruciating pain; he had me trapped in the room and told me not to come out! I was in so much pain, he had to get me to the local hospital.

He instructed me to tell the hospital staff that two girls jumped on me; and he vowed he would *never beat me again*. However, the nurse looked at me suspiciously, but she didn't say anything. I cried silently but had no one I could tell. The nurses placed me on the monitor for a few hours and said our baby was okay! My little baby was a tough cookie, the beating he gave me was deadly. God knew there was powerful young man in my womb.

This happened countless times, especially if he had a bad day! He came home in attack mode. If he wanted to see other women, he would start an argument. It was so bad, that sometimes I started the fights, to get them over with! I became immuned to the beatings.

One day, I snooped through his phone and found out he was in three different relationships. He snatched the phone from me a beat me like never before!

He took me by the hair and slammed me on the bed, and choked me until I was unconscious. Then he split the side of my face and I had to have several stitches. I endured this abuse for six years.

I never thought I would be subject to domestic violence, I never believed *it* would happen to me. The women he cheated with kept coming as we tried to enjoy our son. In some sense I felt trapped, because I didn't want to raise my son alone. So, I put up with a few beatings just to keep my family *together*.

I always imagined myself being married, with perfect children and a home with a white picket fence. I became very insecure and started knocking on women's doors trying to get him to come home.

During this time, I found out he was expecting another child from another girl! I was devastated beyond disbelief. So one night, as I nursed my newborn I got angry all over again. I put my baby in the truck and went searching for him but I didn't find him!

I found one of the women he had impregnated and I followed her! I don't have a clue what was going through my head but I kept riding behind her until we reached her home. She got out and so did I; we exchanged words and began to fight. I finally got up and jumped in my car and sped off because the police were coming. They quickly found me and took me straight to jail.

How could I be so dumb? I thought. While I sat in that cold jail cell [a place I thought I would never be] I was so disappointed with myself. I made bail, but had a felony battery charge and I just knew my life was over! I knew the judge would send me to prison, but God placed an angel in the state attorney office just for me! She arranged a plea deal for me and made me promise that I would never be seen there under those circumstance *again!*

We welcomed the birth of our second child in the midst of this. He was in another relationship and everyone in town knew it. I was so embarrassed but I knew it was something I had to bare to keep my family together. When I came home, I told him that I no longer wanted to be with him… but when I looked around the house, I realized he had already moved his belongings. He cleared the bank accounts and was there to collect the rest of his things. I couldn't believe it; you mean to tell me I don't have the privilege of leaving you!?!

He left me with two children, no vehicle and a rent payment to make on my own. I knew I wanted him to leave; this was what I had prayed for… but I did not expect for my prayers to be answered like *that*.

Chapter 5

It Could Have Been Me

A *man* took me through all these changes and pain… then he left without a single worry! He didn't even worry about the small children he left behind. I prayed for this and specifically asked God to remove anything that was bad for me and my children a few years prior. God always answers our prayers on time!

A few years into the single life, I found out something gravely devastating… Someone I had been closely intimate with had recently been diagnosed with HIV! OMG, did I have *it*!?! How long did he have *it*? Why didn't he tell me? It took me about two weeks before I had enough courage to go to the doctor, and those were the worst and longest two weeks of my life! I felt sick and like I had lost weight, I guess it was all in my head… I didn't lose one pound! I became nauseated and nervous waiting on the Doctor to tell me my HIV status.

I waited and waited a few days went by no news was good news, right? But I needed details… I needed them in black and white. The doctor finally called and asked me to come in. My mind raced and raced until I arrived at the doctor's office to get my results.

Reading the negative result was the best news I had heard in a long time! I breathed a sigh of relief and hugged the doctor so tight. When I walked out I didn't know whether to cry for relief or cry for sorrow. How was I so stupid to trust someone with my life? Nevertheless, I knew this was no one *but* God!

For a few years, I took an HIV test four times a year because I was so scared didn't know if it would show up. Or, maybe just the shock of someone I was actually this close with being diagnosed shook me to the core.

He often told me he was sorry for putting me in a situation like this but I just couldn't face him to talk to about the subject. I was embarrassed for him, in a way... After going back and forth to the doctor for several years he finally sat me down and said, "Cora please stop doing this to yourself get tested once a year use protection and don't live your life in such a dark state." I took heed to his words and only began to go once a year.

    God spared me and I'm forever grateful for His protection from all the dangers I placed myself in! I led a promiscuous lifestyle but God *still* called me HIS! He knew I belonged to Him even when I strayed away and He kept His hands on me! I'm so happy He utilized me for this testimony!

Chapter 6

The Love of Revenge

One would think that the HIV scare would serve as the ultimate reality check… but it birthed something else in me – revenge! Even though those men did not hurt me, I just wanted anyone to feel like I had once felt… betrayed, unwanted, despicable, and unlove! You know the deep hurt a person feels when nothing *seems* to go right. Yes, I know it sounds crazy but in my head my thought process was *right*!

I started dating another man although I was not healed from the hurt of my last relationship. I loved him, but I could never see myself going back to a place of vulnerability… and to be honest, it was familiar and seemed secure because of the toxic mindset I possessed.

I thought "my mentality was *normal* but it really wasn't. The new man opened doors for me and adored my flaws! He massaged my feet and we had deep, meaningful conversations… but something was missing, *he wasn't man enough.*

Man was I going crazy…? I realized, I believed that this man *wasn't* toxic enough for me. I accused him of cheating and having trust issues, I even started a fight… but he definitely was not an abuser. I didn't want to settle down…and deep down inside and that man wanted to marry me but I knew I wasn't ready. I was still confused about what I really wanted. I just wanted to feel love…but now that I had it, I didn't know what to do with it! What was love? Did I even really know the answer to that question? Sadly, I didn't have a clue!

The relationship ended after a few years of forcing something that just wasn't working. I stayed in the relationship just to say I had a man; and my ex-boyfriend didn't want to see me with another man but he didn't want me either! Therefore, he helped ruin the relationship.

That "good" man couldn't take the fact that my ex was so involved in trying to run him away. So, he left. There I was with *another* failed relationship; the adult dating life is a mess [at times]. I vowed that relationships weren't for me *anymore* and I treated men how I believed they treated women! I used them for selfish personal gain [no love]. I had sex for money ONLY and you couldn't talk to me without cash! Was my mother coming out of me? I didn't think about it at the time; I was just so hurt! I guess I could have been called a prostitute, but I didn't look at it that way. I had become so heartless; I didn't even know who I was at the time.

I started a whole business and my body was the product. The clients were few but big in dollars. I was on my high horse young and sexy and used my body as a form of revenge to manipulate and use men. I no longer needed to borrow money… I was the lender and I thought that was something big!

I had my own little operation; I got so carried away that I started my own "services..." If a man needed someone, he would contact me through my connects. I had stripper friends and a few wild ones from going out to the clubs. I met a few girls that I needed on "my team." It was something like a call/escort... but I wasn't a "Madam" [at least I didn't think so]!

The money came faster than I could count... but something was missing! At the end of the day, when I was in my bed alone reality set in! No matter how many men I used or how much money I touched, I was a wreck inside! I had everything I needed, including financial stability... *but* it still wasn't enough!

I even contemplated suicide; I thought overdosing on pills could take it all away! I tried to convince myself that no one would miss me and I told myself that my kids were too young to *really* remember me, if I went now. It thought *this* was the best time to make my exit out of this world.

I behaved as if I were a man stuck in a woman's body. I trusted no one and loved even less at this time of my life!

Then one day, I fell on my knees to pray [desperate & exhausted] … I said, *"Father please take this pain away, only you can do this for me. Heal my broken heart give me the right mind. Neither a man or money can fix this **only** you God."* I cried and prayed everyday until things changed in my mind. When I thought I was getting over on people in my life, *my life* was actually beating me down!

Chapter 7

The Will to Live Again

I quickly learned that my high horse *was not* very stable, and begin I slipped into a deep depression and I stood on a slippery slope. I thought I did everything to avoid going back *that* way.

I kept my house very dark and stayed in my bed most of the time when I was home. Other than going to work, I didn't have any motivation to do much of anything else! To others, I appeared to be happy but at home I was totally different. I often went on social sites for validation because I was popular… when logged-out the depression resurfaced like it never left [because it hadn't]!

I had enrolled to culinary school after my felony charges continued to sabotage my progression! There wasn't much I could do without a clean record. I was already selling dinners and cakes; I just wanted formal training.

I possessed a talent for cooking and it helped me through my depression [so I thought]. I graduated and thought things would get better but it seemed as though things worsened. I had to cut off all my clients and refocus! I really just wanted to be left alone. I returned to work at Burger King and I lived on Section 8. I cried continuously as suicidal thoughts ran through my head over and over.

"This church girl," who was taught how to pray, couldn't seem to bounce back or shake depression. I knew God wouldn't be pleased and I believe I would have gone straight to hell if I had killed myself. I had absolutely nothing going; and once again, I thought about my two kids were better off without me. This was a trick of the enemy that attempted to destroy my life.

I contemplated killing my abuser for many years; he didn't deserve to live! I would kill him first then myself. I felt he wasn't worth the air my children breathed, I thought about poisoning him, shooting him, and/or stabbing him... any type of tragic death seemed fitting. I believed killing him, would make me feel better about killing myself... that way I could see some justice for my life. But God, had alternate plans for my life; He promised he would take care of me, and even in the midst of my "storms," I still believed my faith was high even when I felt low. Deep down I knew I had a purpose but I wasn't sure what it was. Everything seemed dim; my days were long and my nights were even longer… I thank God for a new day!

Chapter 8

Recovery

One day, as I laid in bed... I felt like God himself came down from Heaven just to talk to me; His words were as vivid as the sunlight, "Faith without works is dead!" For some strange reason, although I wasn't connected to God like I should have been, I knew exactly what those words meant! I sat and thought, "God... Who? What? How?"

He gave me three people to call out of the blue and ask for money. I had to face it, I didn't have any money and I wasn't trying to go backwards. I picked up the phone and all three people told me to come pick up the money that I requested!

The day after I made the phone calls, I jumped up and prayed… and I thanked God for His faithfulness. I finally knew it was *Him talking to me*. I immediately got a money order and headed to the court house to pay my restitution fees. This was the "works" part God referred to in our conversation.

After I arrived at the courthouse, I spoke to the clerk, she said I had to wait a few days and everything would be removed from my record! All the charges against me would be eradicated in the system. I was beyond happy; I could get my life back and live *again*.

Once everything was taken care of, I applied for jobs. I knew even with a culinary degree I would still have to start at the bottom; I just wanted better for myself. I began working as a cafeteria worker, for four hours a day. However, I had a goal and I worked hard and within a year, I was in management –YES!! My life was finally going in the *right* direction, I was on track.

I started making good money, I focused on myself and my children. My life was on the up and up. I transitioned into the assistant manager's position, my income increased, and I was finally able to get off Section 8 and food stamps… after 7 long years! With a little faith, work, and God, I was no longer bound by poverty and I felt so good!

My children were on the right track and I returned "to me!" I learned to love and appreciate the person I was becoming.

I was in a good space I could finally see the rainbows that appeared after the storms.

Being an assistant manager was great but deep down inside, I knew I wanted my own business; I wanted to start small and also make a name for myself. I thought, "What can I do?" My mind was so much clearer, so I was open to receive direction from God.

Finally, in 2017, I saw my dreams manifest and I launched my business: "Cora's Cakes and Catering." My vision was in motion and my life was how God purposed it to be. I landed my first big event with more than one hundred people in attendance. Recovery and restoration materialized right before my eyes. I knew it was the Lord's doing!

Chapter 9

New Beginnings

I was on the right path... I became a business owner but if I really wanted my business to take off! So, I had to quit my full-time job as a manager. It was hard but I wanted my business to really flourish as I knew it could! But who would take me more seriously than *myself*?

I was a natural born boss and I knew it. I had been running my own "fake" stores since I was child. I found a part-time overnight job as a CNA to help me out with the expenses of my home. I promoted myself and baked cakes during the day. It was difficult but I didn't lose anything.

My children are doing well despite the absence of their father. I made sure they didn't miss a beat. This was the first time I independently handled the full responsibility of my children without any help! We've travelled and even gone on cruises out of the country. I wanted them to expand their minds to learn and experience the world… Thankfully, I have been able to show them things I wasn't able to see as a child.

Initially, I was scared to raise them on my own… but the experience has been nothing short of amazing. It really has brought out the best in me: the best woman, the best friend, and the best mother/family member I can be.

I grew so much over the years (emotionally, spiritually, financially, and relationally); I didn't allow "menial" things get to me as much as they did before. I was finally at peace. I was even able to gift myself with a trip to Paris, France; a place I've always wanted to go! And I had one of the biggest, most extravagant thirty-fifth birthday parties a young lady could ever imagine! I am even writing a book all about it! God is good, right!!!

I want to help people who have been through similar situations, no matter how big or small. I want people to know that regardless of what's going on we can and will make it through, with the help of God! Look at me, a country girl, from a small town with a big dream! I didn't have any money, but God saw me through everything I went through.

I'm expecting even greater things to come my way after this book. I prayed for "my mind" *daily* and God kept me! He will do everything you ask of Him, if you do what is asked of you… just keep His commandments.

I plan to take more vacations and continue being the best mother I can be! One day soon, I will be open the doors to my own restaurant. Furthermore, I know love will come… but I'm not forcing it. Someone is destined and created just for me *and* my children… and at the right time he will be here! Until then, I'll live life like I should… to the absolute fullest!

Chapter 10

Letters to Beloveds...

My #1 supporters and best friends are my grandmas. I thank you ladies for taking me in when my mother was going through. It takes an undeniably strong person to take on responsibilities that don't belong to them. I thought I was rich because of the way you both took extra good care of me. There was never a need unmet because of you two and all that I am or will ever become, I owe it to God, both of you, and my mother.

Grandma Doritha,

Seeing you now at 98-years-old and no longer able to care for yourself, saddens me, yet, I am honored and privileged to now help take care of you. I wish you could understand what's happening in my life now but you can't. Nevertheless, I know you'd be so proud of me! You bathed me and washed my clothes; even after I had children, you looked out for me. I was your baby and I know you love me; you always treated me well. I love you immensely, grandma; the wrinkles in your skin, your silver hairs and even the way you smile. I really love the woman you are and the friend you have been to me. You taught me how to make beds, cook, and clean. I find myself in your old nightgowns and fussing… just like you! I'm smiling just thinking about the joy you have brought me through the years. I simply want to thank you before you close your eyes and go to be with the Lord. I know, one day... I won't be able to see you anymore here on Earth. But I have no doubts about how much you loved and cared for me. Once again, I thank you and I appreciate you.

Love you always Grandma,

Your Great Granddaughter, Cora.

P.S. Grandma you earned your wings Jan. 25th and you're missed already. See you when I reach our heavenly home...

Grandma Cora,

WOW is all I can say. You gave me your name and all the goodness that makes you, YOU. Even when I need you now, you are right here for me. You are more than just a grandma you are my everything. So strong and beautiful… loving and sensitive. Thanks for treating me like your baby girl and protecting me from all hurt, harm, and danger. Thanks for raising me in the church and teaching me the right way… although I strayed away. You always kept me in your prayers. I know for a fact that you love me; I never questioned your love. I might not tell you all the time, but I truly love you and everything about you. You raised me and taught me how to be a real woman and handle my business. Without you, I would not be the person and mother I am. When I think of you, I think of love. I want my children to feel about me…in the same manner that I feel about you. Thanks for keeping me covered with the blood of Jesus.

    Grandma, I love your whole life; the way you walk, dress, and command the presence of the room. When I enter a room, I want that same aura about myself. I just love that about you grandma. Once again, thank you for everything. I could never repay you, but I just want to appreciate you in this special way. I love you.

Love Your Granddaughter,

Cora

Dear Dad,

First off, thank you for making the best decision for my life that you thought was possible. At age thirty-five, I realize that life is the best thing you both of you gave me. I was blessed with a wonderful home, loving grandmothers that adored me and took care of me. They brought me up the "right way."

Dad, even though; you cannot read this letter or hear me anymore, I'm must be honest… putting you to rest was the hardest thing I ever had to do. I didn't have closure in my heart because we were not on good terms when you transitioned. We had an argument about a week prior to your fatal illness. For weeks I wanted to tell you what was on my mind but I never had the courage to face you. I wanted to tell you so many times that I felt you had failed me by not being there. I thought you should have taken me in when my mom wouldn't, but you were too busy living the life you wanted to live. You hid me from the world and from your family. I was "the child that you had with another woman." You raised children that weren't yours biologically, and I felt like you chose to forsake me. I hurt for a long time and felt betrayed more than anything. I tried to develop a relationship with you, but I was just a child trying to make our relationship "work." I resented you in so many ways. Now you're gone and I should have told you how I felt. I'm sure you loved me but for some reason you couldn't show it. I wish we would have mended our relationship. Now I live the way I wanted "us" to be.

Sincerely,

Your Only Biological Daughter - Cora

Dear Mother:

Thank you. I know I tell you all the time, "Thanks for not throwing me away or being too far gone that you would do any harm to me." That was nothing, but Lord knows I tried to fix you over the years, I know only one person could do that. We have such a wonderful relationship now because it has no lies and we can relate to each other… even though you didn't raise me back in your wild and crazy days.

I am just like you in a good way though. Watching the woman you are growing into makes me proud to have given you a fair chance to make it right with me. Sometimes I want you to settle down and act your age but I have to let you be you because that's what makes you so special to me. I am proud of you and thankful God allowed you to be my mother. I look at all the things you have been through… with drugs and life struggles and I wonder how you got over, but I know it was God! I'm so happy that you were able to recognize that you hurt me and apologized… that took a real woman to do so.

I love you and I will always will express how vital your role as a mother has been in my life. Keep up the good work and keep striving for better; I'm so happy we are in a good place with each other (mentally). God gave us another chance to build and have a solid relationship as a mother and daughter should.

With Love,

Your Daughter - Cora

www.ingramcontent.com/pod-product-compliance
Lightning Source LLC
LaVergne TN
LVHW011857060526
838200LV00054B/4390